a
family
called
Brontë

a
family
called
Brontë

Paula Guzzetti

A People in Focus Book

 **DILLON PRESS**
New York

Maxwell Macmillan Canada
Toronto

Maxwell Macmillan International
New York   Oxford   Singapore   Sydney

Acknowledgments

The author wishes to thank Joyce Stanton, her editor, for her enthusiasm and expertise; Ann Dinsdale of the Brontë Parsonage Museum for her assistance in obtaining photographs; and Kathleen G. Rousseau, professor of English at West Virginia University and honorary American representative of the Brontë Society, for reading the manuscript.

The author extends a very special thank you to Alfred Guzzetti, whose many gifts of Brontëana proved invaluable in the preparation of this work.

A list of illustration sources appears on pages 127-128.

Book design by Carol Matsuyama

Library of Congress Cataloging-in-Publication Data

Guzzetti, Paula.
    A family called Brontë / by Paula Guzzetti. — 1st ed.
      p. cm. — (People in focus series)
    Includes bibliographical references and index.
    Summary: Presents the lives of the talented Brontë family members.
    ISBN 0-87518-592-4
    1. Brontë family—Juvenile literature. 2. Authors, English—19th century—Biography—Juvenile literature. [1. Brontë family. 2. Authors, English.] I. Title. II. Series.
PR4168.G89   1994
823'.809—dc20
[B]   93-8101

Dillon Press   Maxwell Macmillan Canada, Inc.
Macmillan Publishing Company   1200 Eglinton Avenue East
866 Third Avenue   Suite 200
New York, NY 10022   Don Mills, Ontario M3C 3N1

Macmillan Publishing Company is part of the Maxwell Communication Group of Companies.

First edition

Printed in the United States of America

10 9 8 7 6 5 4 3 2 1

To Susan, who made it possible

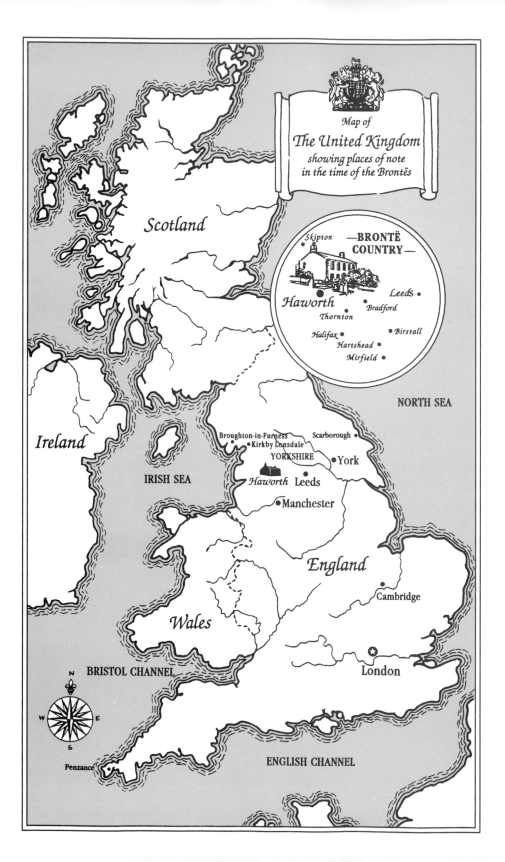

Contents

chapter one

Beginnings

It was a chilly spring day in the year 1820. A group of old wooden carts laden with clothes, household possessions, and a family of eight lumbered up the steep hill that separated the town from the house beyond. Curious and excited, the small children inside viewed the landscape around them with awe. It was all so new and strange, this desolate and barren spot in the north of England that they would call home. They were the Brontë family: Patrick, a parson; his wife, Maria; and their children—Maria, Elizabeth, Charlotte, Branwell, Emily, and Anne. Today we know them as the famous Brontë family of writers, with *Jane Eyre*, *Wuthering Heights*, and *Agnes Grey* three of their most loved and renowned works. But on that April

The Haworth parsonage and church

day, so many years before, they were simply a family, like so many others prior to them and since, preparing to settle into a new home.

The house itself, situated in the village of Haworth, was set on the edge of the Yorkshire moors—miles of gently rolling and unpopulated land that

was snow-covered in winter and alive with sheep, flowers, and birds in summer. Adjoining it, and visible from the windows inside, was a graveyard crowded with large gray tombstones, and a garden with a few scraggly bushes and some grass. Nearby was the church where Mr. Brontë would preach. It could hardly have been a cheerful sight, and never could they have guessed how much it would come to mean to them and to the world in time to follow. Stark and austere, it was also miles and years away from the Brontë family roots.

Patrick Brontë had been born in Ireland forty-three years before. The son of illiterate peasant farmers and the oldest of ten, he had taught himself to read at an early age and by sixteen had found employment as a teacher. Ambitious and eager to learn, he had left Ireland at twenty-five and traveled to England to study theology at Cambridge University. It was during this time that he also changed his name from Brunty to Brontë—a Greek word meaning "thunder"—perhaps in honor of his hero, Lord Nelson, a British naval commander who had been made the Duke of Bronté, or perhaps because of his own fiery nature. Shortly after his graduation in 1806, he was ordained a minister in the Church of England and spent the next six years working in various parts of the country. It was on an assignment in Hartshead, Yorkshire, in 1812, that he first met and fell in love with Maria.

Maria Branwell was from Penzance, a coastal town in the south of England. Gentle and sweet, with a quiet sense of humor, she had come north to visit her cousins, whom Patrick happened to know. Thrown

Patrick Brontë as a young man

Patrick Brontë's birthplace in Ireland

together by chance, Maria and Patrick soon discovered the many interests they had in common, including religion, current affairs and, most important of all in light of the literary children they produced, literature and writing. Both were avid readers. Both loved to write. Though it was Patrick whose poems, articles, and stories eventually made it to print, Maria's letters to Patrick during their courtship and an essay on religion and poverty written during that time reveal her own competence with words. Charlotte Brontë would later write, on reading her mother's letters for the first time years after, that they showed a mind "of a truly fine, pure and elevated order."

Patrick was obviously smitten by this accomplished young woman from the south, and she, by him. In December of 1812, they married.

The first years of their life together were busy and happy. While Mrs. Brontë tended to their home and growing family—their first daughter, Maria, was born in 1813; their second, Elizabeth, two years after—Mr. Brontë fulfilled his many duties as a clergyman—first in Hartshead, where they had settled just after their marriage, and then in Thornton, a town to the north where they moved two years later.

Besides preaching, conducting services, and in-structing the children of the parish in the principles

Maria Branwell (Mrs. Brontë) at age sixteen

of the faith, Mr. Brontë was responsible for the day-to-day welfare of his flock. He visited the sick, offered advice and help to those in need and, because there were no policemen in the towns of England at that time, helped to settle disputes and maintain order. With all he had to do, he also found time to write simple books for the poor and semiliterate so that they, too, could know the joys of reading. He was a firm believer in the power of the written word to enlighten and teach. Perhaps he was remembering his own humble roots.

But life for the Brontës at this time also had its share of fun. Mr. and Mrs. Brontë made many good friends, especially in Thornton, and spent many pleasant hours attending parties, concerts, and dinners at the homes of some of the town's most prominent residents.

And it was also in Thornton that their next four and most famous children were born: Charlotte—passionate, determined and, through her novels, a voice for the equality of women—on April 21, 1816; Branwell, their only son—brilliant and restless, with all of his father's energy and fire—on June 26, 1817; Emily—aloof and independent, with a soul as vast as the open moors she came to love—on July 30, 1818; and Anne—gentle and sweet like her mother, and the

most religious of the four—on January 17, 1820.

The Brontës were happy in Thornton and might have stayed there forever had not Mr. Brontë, always eager for advancement, seized the opportunity for a better post.

Shortly after Anne's birth, the trustees of St. Michael and All Angels Church in Haworth offered him a position as the church's curate. Though the move would mean living in the windy and freezing north, far from their many friends and the life they enjoyed, Mr. Brontë felt it was an offer he could not refuse.

The pay would be better—an important consideration for a husband and father of six. The house would be bigger and would be theirs, rent-free. And the position at St. Michael's would be his for life.

It wouldn't be easy. The move itself would involve an exhausting, day-long journey across rough terrain. Mrs. Brontë, still weak from childbirth, would need looking after. And baby Anne, so delicate and small, would require extra care. But he was ready for the challenge.

He had come a long way. He had worked hard to make his place in the world. He had established his reputation as a man of character and strength. And, he was a Brontë!

Strong and determined as ever, Patrick led his wife

The Brontë home in Thornton, England, where Charlotte, Branwell, Emily, and Anne were born.

The parsonage at Haworth as it looked in the Brontës' time

and young family to the lonely parsonage on the moors—the home where his talented offspring would achieve fame—the home where the story of the Brontë children begins.

chapter two

A Sad Time

To Maria, who was six, and Elizabeth, who was five, the parsonage at Haworth must have offered wonderful possibilities. With its many rooms and spacious setting, there would be lots of places to explore and lots of spots where they could play. Though Charlotte, Branwell, Emily, and Anne were too young to appreciate it just then, they, too, would soon discover the hidden joys of their moorland home.

The moors extended as far back as the eye could see, uninterrupted by tall buildings or trees. Though an occasional cottage dotted the landscape, sending up curls of black smoke into the open sky, the land belonged much more to nature than to man. It could be a harsh and dangerous place in winter when the

The Haworth moors in winter

gusty northern winds whipped the falling snow into drifts as high as a man's head. But it had a kind of peace and tranquil beauty in summer, the children's favorite time.

In those warmer and more gentle months, sheep wandered among the hills and valleys in leisurely pursuit of their next grassy meal. Deer darted this way and that to the songs of the moor larks above. Butter-

flies flitted in and out among the stalks of fragrant heather, adding dashes of white and yellow to the purple blaze. And tiny brooks, frozen solid just weeks before, bubbled with life. To the children, especially Emily, who would later set so much of her writing on the moors, it must have seemed like a backyard made in heaven.

And if the house itself lacked luxury, the children

didn't mind. Sparsely furnished—partly due to the family's small income and partly due to Mr. Brontë's preference for simplicity—it had its own share of special places and favorite spots: the tiny room on the second floor that the children took over as their study, the kitchen with its blazing hearth fire that warmed them on freezing-cold Yorkshire nights, the dining room where in later years they would gather to write.

And it was also rich in what the family loved most: Magazines, newspapers, and books were in abundance. Like Mr. Brontë, the children learned to read early and from the very beginning were given free access to all of the literary material in the house. They read the news, the Bible, and the works of major writers, including the novels of Sir Walter Scott, the poetry of Lord Byron, and the plays of William Shakespeare. Unlike other parents of the day, Mr. Brontë believed that children should be heard as well as seen and encouraged them to talk about what they read, both to him and to one another. As a result, even when they were very young, they were expressing thoughtful opinions on literature and world affairs. He was understandably proud of his bright and informed brood. But Mrs. Brontë never really got a chance to enjoy them.

Just nine months after the family's move to Haworth, Maria Brontë became gravely ill. Confined to her bed,

The parsonage dining room

she was cared for in the long months that followed by her husband, who stayed close by her side, and her sister, Elizabeth Branwell, who had come north from Penzance to help. Left to themselves while the adults in the household tended to their mother's needs, the children clung together in silence, sensing the seriousness of their mother's condition and dreading what might come. In September of 1821, their worst fears were realized. Maria Brontë died and was buried shortly after, in the church across from their home.

Mr. Brontë was beside himself with grief. Leaving

the children in the care of their aunt, he went off to his study to sit alone. Though Aunt Branwell did her best to take care of them in his absence, she did not have the kind and loving ways of her sister. Surprisingly, it was seven-year-old Maria who took charge, assuming the role of mother to her younger siblings and offering them the love and comfort they now lacked. The children worshiped her, and Branwell especially adored her. With her help, they slowly began to get over a very difficult time.

But if Aunt Branwell had any thoughts of returning to her beloved Penzance after her sister's death, those thoughts were soon erased from her mind. Though she disliked the severe climate of the north and missed her many friends in the south, her strong sense of duty to her sister's family kept her at Haworth for the rest of her life. And though the children never really loved her, they did come to appreciate her efforts on their behalf. She managed the household well, taught the girls to clean and sew, and soon became an important link in the Brontë family chain.

Of course Mr. Brontë, aware of his duty to his family, realized that he could not mourn forever, and as time passed, his thoughts turned once again to his children. With his wife's death and his own advancing age, he knew that they might soon have to face the world

A silhouette of Aunt Branwell

on their own. Formal schooling was crucial. But in those days before free public education, schooling cost money—money that Mr. Brontë didn't have.

The solution seemed to come in the form of the Clergy Daughters' School at Cowan Bridge, a tiny village near Kirkby Lonsdale. It was a new school, and

although it had the advantage of being free for the
daughters of clergymen, it was also fifty long miles
from Haworth. The older girls would go there—Maria,
Elizabeth, Charlotte, and Emily were enrolled in 1824
at the ages of ten, nine, eight, and six—and Branwell,
now seven, would study at home with his father, whose
Cambridge education and gentle view of childhood
made him a natural teacher.

But things didn't work out at all as Mr. Brontë had
expected. Cowan Bridge turned out to be a miserable
place—cold, damp, with inadequate food and a supervisor who was strict and unkind—very much like Lowood,
the school that Charlotte later immortalized in her
novel *Jane Eyre*.

Within a year after arriving, Maria fell ill with
tuberculosis and died. A few weeks later, Elizabeth also
succumbed. Mr. Brontë was devastated. Immediately
setting off for Cowan Bridge, he brought Charlotte and
Emily home, determined that, forever after, his four
remaining children would be in his care alone.

The family had suffered two more brutal blows.
Losing Elizabeth was hard. But for the children, especially Branwell, the loss of Maria was like the death of
their mother all over again.

The tragedy brought the four young Brontës together as never before. Turning away from the outside

The Clergy Daughters' School at Cowan Bridge

world, becoming even more dependent on one another for love and support, they spent all of their time together—reading, talking, helping with the household chores, and taking long and vigorous walks on the moors.

They also spent hours at their studies. Their lessons, now almost solely in the hands of their father and aunt, included literature, history, geography, grammar, and religion. A local artist and musician were brought in to teach painting, drawing, piano, organ, and flute. In addition, Branwell studied Latin and Greek and became so fluent in each that he could write them simultaneously—Latin with one hand and Greek with the other. He later invented a language of his own—a mixture of Cornish, Irish, Latin, and the English dialect of the Yorkshire region—

which he and his sisters learned to speak.

Words of all kinds were of the utmost importance in the children's lives. It was through reading, writing, and the sharing of feelings and thoughts that they began to recover from a period of deep and tragic loss.

It was around this time that a new and joyous presence was added to the household. In 1825, Tabitha Aykroyd, or Tabby as the children called her, came to work in the Brontë home. A widow with no children of her own, Tabby devoted herself wholeheartedly to the Brontë family from the day she arrived until her death thirty years later—cooking, cleaning, and taking charge of the household with all the roughness and love of a country mother.

Even more to the children's delight, she told wonderful stories. A local woman, born and raised in Yorkshire, Tabby knew the area and its people as only a native could and brought along to the parsonage, in addition to her maternal and domestic skills, a supply of local folklore and gossip.

The children teased her and loved her and spent many nights huddled by the kitchen fire captivated by her tales. She was a breath of life and love in a family that badly needed it. She was also an inspiration for the four budding writers in her charge. For the Brontë children, it was the beginning of a happier time.

chapter three

Imaginary Worlds

For the next four years, the young Brontës lived as much in the lively world of imagination as they did in the real world of Haworth. These were the years when their passion for writing took flight.

It all started with a gift presented to Branwell by his father one June day in 1826, when Branwell was eight. Mr. Brontë had been away on church business and had returned home with presents for the children—among them a toy village for the girls and a box of twelve wooden soldiers for Branwell. Because the children were asleep, he had left the gifts beside their beds, hoping to surprise them in the morning.

Not only were the children surprised, they were delighted. The gifts were a big success, but the toy

soldiers were the favorite. Branwell generously offered
to share his new treasures with his sisters, and soon
each child had chosen the soldier he or she liked best.
The children named them, made up stories about them,
and used them over and over again in their play. They
knew from their reading that the adventures of real
soldiers were often chronicled in newspapers and
books, and it wasn't long before they were recording the
adventures of their own toy men in tiny volumes of their
own making—some not much bigger than postage
stamps.

On small scraps of paper stitched together by hand
and in writing so minute as to be practically micro-
scopic, they began their story of "The Twelves"—as the
soldiers came to be called—complete with histories,
essays, songs, illustrations, and maps of the imaginary
kingdom of Glasstown, where the stories were set. With
Charlotte and Branwell leading the way, they poured all
of their energies and talents into the work, producing
torrents of words and becoming so deeply involved in
the Glasstown world that they could hardly think about
anything else. "Scribblemania" was what Branwell later
jokingly called it.

But scribblemania turned out to be far more than
mere child's play. It was, along with reading, the way
the Brontë children learned to write. The intense collab-

The juvenile books, photographed with a coin to give a sense of their size

oration and the constant manipulation of words proved as instructive as any teacher, and the techniques they acquired during those days of group authorship were subsequently transferred to their individual work. No wonder Charlotte later admitted that the pen that had produced her world-renowned novels—*The Professor, Jane Eyre, Shirley,* and *Villette*—had been busy before. For all of the Brontë children, scribblemania helped pave the way for the famous poems and stories that followed.

Looking at the tiny books today, with their eye-straining pages and all-but-indecipherable print, we can only guess at why the children chose to work so small. Though the idea of such little books is certainly intriguing, the task itself must have been patience-trying and slow.

Perhaps paper was scarce or too expensive for them to buy in large amounts.

Perhaps the books were designed to fit into the hands of the toy soldiers that had inspired them.

Or maybe secrecy was at work. No one except the four children themselves knew about the tales and, should anyone have found them, the tiny writing would have made them almost impossible to read. That thought alone must have caused the children endless delight.

As the years passed and the stories took new and unexpected turns, Emily and Anne eventually decided to leave the saga to their older brother and sister and branch off on their own. Glasstown had by then been superseded by its offshoot kingdom called Angria, and the focus had shifted away from the original "Twelves" to more aristocratic ladies and lords. The two younger girls, more in tune with the everyday life of Yorkshire than with the distant world of nobility, set off for Gondal—the rough and wild land they created together, very much like their Yorkshire home.

In stories and poems set against the harsh and

beautiful landscape they loved so well, they chronicled the lives and loves of the Gondal people—plain, simple folk, full of the gruffness and fire of the Yorkshire locals.

And where Angria had been dominated by men— the Duke of Zamorna and the Earl of Northangerland were its chief players and rivals—Gondal was placed firmly in the hands of a female: Augusta Geraldine Almeda, as she was called, partly inspired by Victoria, the young princess of England, soon to become queen.

Though the Gondal stories no longer exist (they were either lost or destroyed years later), we know from the poetry that remains, and a diary letter of Emily's, that the Gondal world was as real to Emily and Anne as Haworth itself.

For Charlotte and Branwell, the fictional world of Angria was even more vivid and true—so true, in fact, that they portrayed it in pictures. In elaborate watercolors and drawings done with the same painstaking attention to detail that characterized their writing, they set down the people and places they saw in their minds—the great cities, the heroes, the grand duke himself. The often-grim scenes just outside their Haworth home—the gray church, the graveyard, the lonely moors beyond—were transformed in their art into the shimmering lands of their dreams.

But those magical days were shortly to end. In

Charlotte's "English Lady"—possibly used as an Angrian illustration

1830, when the children's productivity was at its height, Mr. Brontë became dangerously ill. His lungs were congested, and he had difficulty breathing. Death in the parsonage seemed once more a grim possibility. Not all the imagination in the world could ease the children's fears, for this time there was even more than the life of a family member at stake.

If Mr. Brontë died, the Haworth curacy would go to someone else, and the parsonage would go with it. The four parentless children would be left without a home, without income, and without any means of providing for themselves.

Fortunately, Mr. Brontë recovered. But the close call would leave him forever cautious about his health.

He took to wrapping great quantities of cloth around his neck to protect himself from drafts. He ate his meals alone in his study to avoid distractions that might hinder digestion. And, except for brief exchanges with his children, he withdrew more and more from the family scene.

But though he grew physically remote, he never stopped worrying about his children.

His illness had made him realize again that Charlotte, Branwell, Emily, and Anne had to be prepared for the future. But formal schooling, so necessary for employment, was still an expense he couldn't afford.

Branwell's drawing of the Duke of Zamorna

This time some old friends from years back offered
to help. A new boarding school for girls had recently
opened near the home of the Rev. and Mrs. Atkinson,
Charlotte's godparents from Thornton. Housed in a
country mansion called Roe Head, in the village of
Mirfield, it was run by a Miss Margaret Wooler. A kind
and educated woman, Miss Wooler was well suited to
the task. Unlike the cold and hard supervisor of Cowan
Bridge, she cared about the girls in her charge and
treated them with consideration and respect. In addition to instruction in the basic academic subjects, she
saw to their physical well-being, making sure they got

plenty of good food, fresh air, exercise, and rest— quite a contrast to Cowan Bridge, where the health of growing girls was not merely neglected but deliberately ignored.

But also unlike Cowan Bridge, which was free to the daughters of clergymen, Roe Head cost money. Sympathetic to the family's financial plight and to the children's need for formal schooling, the Atkinsons generously offered to pay Charlotte's way, with the understanding that, as the oldest, she would instruct her younger brother and sisters upon her return.

Though Charlotte appreciated the kind offer and was eager for a more formal education, the thought of outside schooling was understandably troubling. She had no way of knowing how different Roe Head would be from Cowan Bridge—that nightmarish institution from the past that had killed her two sisters.

Even more, the idea of leaving home and her family and the imaginary world she had shared with Branwell, Emily, and Anne filled her with despair.

There would be no more whispered meetings about characters and plots, no more secret adventures in kingdoms far beyond. The collaboration would end. After four years of fantasy and fun, the real world had not only intruded, but triumphed.

chapter four

Off to School

In January of 1831, fourteen-year-old Charlotte Brontë said a tearful good-bye to her family and set off for Miss Wooler's school at Roe Head. It was one of the most difficult and courageous acts of her life. In addition to her painful memories of Cowan Bridge and her sadness at leaving Haworth, she was shy. Except for that brief period of schooling when she was eight, she had reached adolescence without the usual outside contacts and with no friends except her brother and sisters. Suddenly she found herself thrust into the midst of strangers in a place far from home. No wonder Ellen Nussey found her crying in a schoolroom corner the day of her arrival.

Ellen was a girl about Charlotte's age who was also

Charlotte's drawing of Miss Wooler's school at Roe Head

new at Roe Head, having arrived just the week before. Kind and gentle, she was deeply touched by Charlotte's tears; and, homesick herself, she understood Charlotte's distress. She approached Charlotte to offer comfort and support, and it wasn't long before the two unhappy girls were weeping in each other's arms. It was the beginning of a friendship that would last through Charlotte's life—one of three she made at Roe Head; but of the three, it was the most important—and the most surprising—because Charlotte and Ellen had so little in common.

Although Ellen was loyal and sweet, she was neither brilliant nor clever. She had none of Charlotte's poetry or spirit and, by Charlotte's own later accounts, was often lifeless and dull.

Her background and circumstances were also very different from Charlotte's. Like the other girls in the school, Ellen came from a family with connections and money. Her home, about ten miles away in the village of Birstall, was comfortable and large with lovely grounds, fine old trees, and many of the luxuries the parsonage lacked. It was "paradise" according to Branwell, who later visited it with Charlotte, befitting the proper, affluent, though unexciting family that inhabited it.

But Charlotte and Ellen "suited"—to use Charlotte's word. And though Charlotte never shared her fantasy world with Ellen, thinking Ellen wouldn't understand, she found in her friend's goodness and loyalty the support she needed. Long after their school days, the two girls remained in close contact through visits and letters—some four hundred of which Ellen lovingly preserved. We have Ellen to thank, for much of what we know about Charlotte and her family comes from that long and cherished correspondence.

Despite their lifelong ties, however, it was probably during those early days at Roe Head that Ellen's friendship meant the most, particularly because Charlotte seemed so unapproachable and strange to the

Charlotte's drawing of Ellen Nussey as a young woman

other girls. In her unfashionable country clothes, with her thick Irish accent and her serious manner, she was far removed from her more stylish and light-hearted classmates. Her preference for solitary walks, her dedication to her studies, and her extraordinary knowledge of literature and world affairs only helped to widen the gap.

Fortunately, among the ten girls in attendance, there was another who not only shared Charlotte's passions but went far beyond. Her name was Mary Taylor, and she would become Charlotte's second lifelong friend.

Mary came from a large, well-informed, and well-read family like Charlotte's. Lively and opinionated, she, too, had been influenced by her father, a manufacturer by trade who had read and traveled widely and had filled his home with books and paintings and objects from abroad. Like Mr. Brontë, Mr. Taylor had instilled in his children a love of politics and the arts and had given them free rein in the expression of their thoughts.

But where Charlotte's family discussed, Mary's family argued.

And while Charlotte's took a moderate to conservative stand on the issues of the day, Mary's viewed the world through the radical eyes of nonconformists.

The Taylor household was noisy, often wild, and

always bursting with life, a marked contrast to the overwhelming quiet of Haworth. Despite her shyness, Charlotte came to enjoy her later visits to the Taylor home, finding in Mary and her family the stimulation she craved.

Charlotte spent eighteen months at Roe Head, winning, over time, not only the affection of her two new friends but also the admiration of her teachers and the respect of her fellow students. When she left in July of 1832, she took along prizes for her achievements; a well-deserved reputation as a storyteller (her ghost tales at bedtime left her roommates screaming in terror); and a deep and lifelong attachment to Miss Wooler, her teacher and third Roe Head friend. She returned home with a feeling of confidence that was both gratifying and new. She had not only survived her time away from Haworth; she had actually enjoyed it.

Equipped now to earn her way as a governess (one of the few occupations open to women), she delayed seeking employment until she had instructed her sisters in the subjects she had mastered. Turning the dining room into their study, the three girls worked diligently at their tasks. It was a happy time for them, and for Branwell, too, for while Charlotte, Emily, and Anne made plans for their careers in teaching, Branwell was busily preparing for his future in art.

Multitalented as he was—with his wit, gift of gab, and aptitude for languages, writing, music, and drawing—Branwell could have pursued any one of a number of fields. But an 1834 exhibition of works by his teacher, William Robinson, an accomplished portraitist, convinced him that his heart and his livelihood could be best served through painting.

He began to work seriously in oils, producing a study of himself and his sisters the following year. (He later painted himself out, leaving a yellowish streak where he had stood.) But his dream of attending London's famous Royal Academy of Arts seemed remote until Charlotte, in genuine sisterly fashion, found a way to make it come true.

In 1835, Charlotte was invited back to Roe Head to teach—an invitation that was not only flattering but also practical. In exchange for her services, which Miss Wooler highly prized, Charlotte would receive a modest salary—enough to subsidize Branwell in London— along with free tuition at Roe Head for Emily. Happy to be able to provide for her brother's and sister's schooling and thrilled at the idea of returning to Roe Head as part of Miss Wooler's staff, Charlotte accepted the offer.

But what had sounded so promising proved a disaster. Charlotte discovered, to her dismay, that the

Branwell's portrait of his sisters: Charlotte, Emily, and Anne

demands of classroom teaching were completely alien to her nature. It was one thing to instruct her sisters in the quiet and leisure of home. It was quite another to take on a roomful of strange girls and to try to fit into the established Roe Head routine. She loathed the work and would gladly have given up and returned to Haworth had not her strong sense of duty forced her to persevere. It was a difficult time, made all the more trying because, in addition to her own miseries, she was deeply concerned about Emily.

Even more than Charlotte, Emily longed to return home. The change from her own free and unrestricted existence to the rigors of boarding-school life was more than she could handle. Though she made a brave and valiant effort to struggle on with her studies, the strain had soon taken its toll. She grew thin and pale and so desperately homesick that, after a mere three months, Charlotte arranged for her withdrawal. She returned to Haworth in October of 1835, happy to be free.

For Emily, home was not just the place she loved most in the world. Home was where she had to be to survive. A true child of the moors, Emily depended on the space and seclusion of Haworth for her very existence. There, on the vast and open lands that she cherished, she could feel nature at its purest and most intense. To Emily, every blade of grass, every sprig of heather, every cloud in the open sky signaled an awesome and wondrous presence.

Not religious in the usual sense, despite her father's vocation and her own Christian upbringing, she neither prayed nor attended church. What she did instead was rather extraordinary. In total seclusion—in the pitch blackness and profound silence of the moorland nights—Emily and the universe became one.

It is a difficult thing to understand, this special power that Emily possessed. Few people, particularly in the West, where individuals, events, and natural occurrences tend to be viewed on the surface and in isolation, have even attempted what Emily regularly achieved. Through an intense and total concentration on the vast emptiness around her, Emily entered a trancelike state in which she neither saw, heard, nor felt the sights, sounds, and sensations of the real world as we know it. She lost all awareness of her physical self. What she found instead was something much greater—not God in the Christian sense, nor even a presence that had any recognizable form or shape, but the unseen and all-powerful force that flows through all things and gives them life. It was as if all the separate elements of the universe—the earth, the trees, the stars, the sky, the life force itself—had merged into one, with one common heartbeat and pulse, and she had become part of it.

It was this all-encompassing view of life and the cosmos that inspired every word of her poetry and fiction. Those magical moments—fleeting though they were and so entirely dependent on the moorland setting—were crucial to her writing and her survival. Though Charlotte probably didn't understand the full intensity of Emily's experiences when she arranged for her to return home, she knew that away from the moors Emily might die.

As for Branwell, though he made it to London, he never set foot in the Royal Academy. For reasons that are not clear, he returned to Haworth in humiliation and shame ten days after his departure.

Whether he lost confidence in his own ability so far from the love and support of home, whether he was overwhelmed by the noisy and bustling city on his first and only visit, whether he was actually robbed of his money as he later reported, his failure to follow through on his dream filled him with lifelong despair. He had disappointed his family, who had struggled on his behalf. It was a blow to his image and self-esteem from which he never recovered.

Surprisingly, it was Anne—gentle and sweet though she was—who fared best, going on to Roe Head in Emily's place and remaining as a student for an impressive two-and-a-half years.

Branwell's caricature of himself

But though Charlotte and Anne at least managed to cope, they were no happier during their time away from Haworth than Branwell or Emily had been. By 1838, Charlotte's low spirits and Anne's failing health had caused them, too, to give up and return home.

And yet, despite their unhappiness and failures, none of the Brontë children was ready to admit defeat. Though they longed to remain at home, the thundering Brontë name guaranteed that they would each venture forth again.

chapter five

Out in the World

When Branwell returned from London, with his art career in question, he found himself thinking again about writing. Resuming work on the Angrian stories, he began to consider writing as a possible profession and sent out letters of inquiry to publishers and authors. Several went to the editor of *Blackwood's Magazine*—a parsonage favorite—detailing his qualifications for a position on the magazine's staff. Another went to the poet William Wordsworth, whom Mr. Brontë especially admired, asking for help in launching a writing career. But none of his letters was answered, which just added to his despair.

Aware of his suffering, Mr. Brontë arranged for Branwell to resume painting lessons with William

Robinson, and shortly after, plans were made for him to earn his living as a portrait painter in nearby Bradford, a local center for aspiring artists and writers. With financial help from Aunt Branwell, he was set up in rooms and a studio with the hope that commissioned portraits would provide the means for his future support.

But with so many painters competing in one place, there simply wasn't enough work to go around. Though Branwell did some studies of his landlord and several portraits of Bradford's more influential residents, he could not get enough work to sustain him. After about a year, he was forced to pack up and return home.

Meanwhile, Emily, despite her near-fatal experience at Roe Head, had found herself a teaching position at Law Hill, a girls' boarding school near Halifax, about twenty miles from Haworth. It was grueling work—"from six in the morning until near eleven at night," according to Charlotte in a letter to Ellen. She stayed on for a commendable six months before she, too, returned home.

Charlotte and Anne took a different course. Though Charlotte had also considered a writing career and had sent out her own share of inquiry letters, she received a reply from Robert Southey, the poet laureate of England, that confirmed her suspicions

Branwell's portrait of his Bradford landlord

about her chances in the field.

"Literature cannot be the business of a woman's life," Southey had written back, expressing in nine infuriating words the prevailing view of the time. Though Charlotte certainly did not agree, she was realistic enough about the world to understand the obstacles that would be placed in her path and practical enough about her financial situation to know that she must pursue the expected course. So she and Anne became governesses, not an easy or pleasant choice of work.

For one thing, a governess had to live in her employer's home, no matter how attached she was to her own. There was no returning to her own familiar surroundings at the end of each day—no weekends or holidays off to spend with her family. Governessing meant a twenty-four-hour-a-day, day-after-day commitment to her employer's children, whom she was expected to educate and amuse. Her own feelings and needs were secondary.

For another, though a governess assumed full responsibility for the children in her care, she had no authority or status in the household. She was viewed as hired help—to be tolerated by the parents, ignored by their servants and guests, and abused by the children, who often did their best to irritate her and drive her away. With no companionship or support, a governess quickly learned to devise her own methods by which to cope. But the constant struggle took its toll, depressing her spirits and depleting her strength.

And for all her efforts and sacrifice, she was grossly underpaid. The typical Victorian governess earned about forty pounds a year, the equivalent of seventy-five dollars. Even in those times, when wages and prices were far lower than they are today, the sum was considered a pittance.

It was with this grim picture in mind that Charlotte and Anne, desperate for work, embarked on their governessing careers.

In April of 1839, Anne took up residence with a family Miss Wooler knew in Mirfield called the Inghams, becoming governess to their two older children. In a letter home shortly after, she described her pupils as "little dunces," unable to read and hopelessly out of control. Expected to deal with their atrocious behavior on her own, she resorted to the equally outrageous measures later described in *Agnes Grey.* Who would have thought that the kind and gentle daughter of a parson could have shoved children and pulled hair! She was dismissed in December of 1840.

Meanwhile, Charlotte, also by way of Miss Wooler, had secured a position with the Sidgwick family of

Stonegappe, near Skipton. In a letter to Ellen a month after her arrival, she described six-year-old Matilda and four-year-old John Benson as "riotous," "perverse," and "unmanageable" and complained bitterly about Mrs. Sidgwick's lack of kindness to her. She left after two months.

And things were no better for Branwell, who, like his sisters, was also unhappily employed. With his dream of a career in the arts seeming more and more hopeless, he had set off for distant Broughton-in-Furness to serve as a tutor to the sons of the wealthy Postlethwaite family. Unable to get Angria out of his mind, he had spent so much of the boys' instruction time drawing pictures and telling stories that he was fired—his third embarrassing failure in the space of four years.

It was a difficult time for all the young Brontës, and the prospects of their ever finding agreeable work seemed increasingly dim. Fortunately, there was home— the safe and welcoming haven to which they returned between attempts at employment.

And the parsonage was an unusually lively place during those years between 1838 and 1842 when they reassembled. Charlotte's friend Mary Taylor came, bringing along her younger sister Martha, who not only charmed everyone with her chatter but flirted with Branwell. Ellen Nussey visited—always a cheering presence for all of the Brontës, who liked her enormously. And, best of all, Willy Weightman came to stay.

The Reverend William Weightman was the handsome, dedicated, and fun-loving curate whom Mr. Brontë had hired as his assistant. Just twenty-five when he arrived at the parsonage in August of 1839, he caused quite a stir among the usually sedate Brontë sisters, who pretended indifference in his presence but talked of little else behind his back. Dubbed "Miss Celia Amelia" because of his pink skin and auburn curls, the new curate quickly became a favorite. He proved a devoted helpmate to Mr. Brontë, a friend to Branwell, a respectful companion to Aunt Branwell, and a source of continual excitement and fascination to the young women.

An outrageous flirt, he devoted his attentions to each of them in turn, causing Charlotte to alternately praise and condemn him, Emily to grow less aloof, and poor Anne to fall in love. Willy Weightman was a tease, already engaged to a girl back home. When he toyed with their affections, it never occurred to him that one of them might take him seriously.

But though Anne would later suffer because of her feelings for him, life at the parsonage during those days of his curacy was at its most lighthearted and social. The young Brontës and their new friend took long noisy walks together, attended lectures in a nearby town, and talked endlessly into the night. The playful Willy even sent the girls anonymous valentines, trudging a distance of ten miles to post them so as not to be discovered.

But despite William Weightman's universal appeal, the Brontës' attempts at outside employment continued. By the spring of 1841, Anne had settled in with the Robinson family of Thorp Green, near York, where she remained for the next four years; Branwell was working as a railroad clerk, though he was later dismissed for careless recordkeeping (his account books were full of Angrian poems and drawings); and Charlotte had become governess to the White family of Leeds. Emily, by mutual consent, remained at home, assisting with the household chores and dreaming of Gondal—the only one of the Brontë children who was completely content. Emily was free—free to write, free to dream, free to attain those spiritual heights. If only Charlotte, Branwell, and Anne could have joined her.

In May of 1841, while working in Leeds, Charlotte had an idea that she thought would make that possible. Shortly after, with special permission from the Whites, she traveled home to Haworth to share it with her family.

chapter six

A Troubled Time

Charlotte's plan, to which her family agreed, was for them to open a school of their own. There were two possible sites: Miss Wooler's now-abandoned building at Roe Head, which Charlotte's former teacher had generously offered her, or the parsonage itself. By becoming their own employers, they would be free to arrange their own schedules and workloads and would no longer be subject to outside restrictions and demands.

Aware that foreign travel and study would enhance their credentials, Charlotte believed that they should first spend some time abroad. In February of 1842, with Anne still employed at Thorp Green, Charlotte set off for Belgium with Emily, where they enrolled at the Pensionnat Heger, a girls' boarding school in Brussels.

Charlotte's choice of city, companion, and school had, not surprisingly, been carefully thought out.

Brussels had been chosen on the recommendation of Mary Taylor's family, some of whom were either visiting or studying there. (Mary and her brother Joe were touring the city. Martha was attending school.)

Emily had been chosen over Anne to give her one last chance at formal schooling, although it must have taken all of Charlotte's powers of persuasion to convince her to go along.

And the Pensionnat Heger was selected because it offered the advanced study of French, German, and Italian necessary for a well-balanced continental education at a relatively low cost. With Aunt Branwell financing tuition and board, Charlotte was considerately frugal.

For the next nine months, the two determined sisters devoted themselves wholeheartedly to their studies, forgetting that they were strangers in a foreign country, that they were—at the ages of twenty-six and twenty-four—considerably older than their Belgian schoolmates, and that the parsonage was hundreds of miles away. Though Emily, silent and distant, spoke to no one except Charlotte for the entire length of their

The Pensionnat Heger in Brussels, where Charlotte and Emily studied

stay, she worked "like a horse," to use Charlotte's phrase, and came to excel in French, German, piano, and drawing.

As for Charlotte, who had always loved learning, those early months at the Pensionnat were especially happy. Although she may not have realized it then, she was slowly falling in love.

The object of Charlotte's affections was Monsieur Constantin Heger, the dark and fiery professor of French literature with whom she was studying, who also happened to be married to the school's proprietress. Kind and gentle underneath, Monsieur Heger hid his true nature behind a frightening facade, assuming an exterior gruffness and harsh teaching manner that kept the more indifferent pupils on their toes, and left the others in a state of tears—all, that is, except Charlotte.

Charlotte, every bit Monsieur Heger's intellectual and emotional match, saw through his facade. Understanding the reason for his tyrannical methods, but never once letting on, she played along, resorting to sobs at his outbursts like the rest of the girls.

But unlike the others, who cared little for learning and even less for the professor, Charlotte was passionate about both. She soon blossomed under the strict tutelage to earn the professor's special attention and esteem.

It wasn't long before she was being showered with small kindnesses: his handkerchief to dry her

tears, gifts of books left discreetly in her desk, and
the very flattering request that she give him lessons
in English (which she did)—all under the disapprov-
ing eye of his wife, who said nothing but secretly
plotted revenge.

Then suddenly, in mid-September of 1842 when
Charlotte and Emily were well into their work, they
received the shocking news that Willy Weightman
was dead—a victim of the cholera epidemic that was
sweeping through Haworth. The dreaded disease, all
but unheard of in the developed countries of the
world today, was one of many that threatened the
village's earlier inhabitants. Spread by poor sanitation
and contaminated food and water supplies, it struck
the young curate at his compassionate best, as he was
fulfilling his parish duties and making the rounds of
the sick.

Charlotte and Emily were deeply saddened by his
loss. But Branwell and Anne were devastated.

Already despondent over the course his own life
had taken, Branwell sought comfort for the death of his
friend in alcohol and drugs.

And grief-stricken Anne, far away at Thorp Green,
mourned his loss in lonely silence—struggling on through
her pain, trying desperately to cope.

It was only later, almost two years after Willy's

death, that she put her feelings into words, in a gentle tribute in verse:

> Yes, thou art gone! and never more
>   Thy sunny smile shall gladden me;
> But I may pass the old church door,
>   And pace the floor that covers thee,
>
> May stand upon the cold, damp stone,
>   And think that, frozen, lies below
> The lightest heart that I have known,
>   The kindest I shall ever know.

And true to the sad pattern of the Brontës' lives, hardly had they recovered from one tragedy when another cruelly followed. Two months after Willy Weightman's death, Aunt Branwell became gravely ill. Leaving their studies, Charlotte and Emily rushed home to Haworth only to arrive too late. The woman who had raised them in their mother's place had died two days before.

The grim turn of events necessitated an immediate change of plan. With Aunt Branwell gone and Tabby too old to manage the household alone, one of the girls had to remain at home. The obvious choice was Emily. With thoughts of the professor drawing her back, Charlotte returned to Brussels alone.

Then something had to be done about Branwell, whose wretched state was becoming increasingly worrisome. This time it was Anne who took charge, arranging for Branwell to join her at Thorp Green as tutor to the Robinsons' sons.

And a new curate had to be found to assist Mr. Brontë in Willy Weightman's place. A three-year-long search would bring the Reverend Arthur Bell Nicholls to Haworth—a man of character and strength who was to have a profound effect on the family's lives.

But fate had yet to deliver its final blow. Charlotte found, upon her return to Brussels, that a troubling change had taken place in her relationship with her teacher. The man who had given her his special consideration and time—who had taught her, befriended her, and made her life in a foreign land rewarding and happy—had suddenly grown distant and remote. He was now entirely absorbed by new and consuming tasks that left him little time for her.

Charlotte was part of the faculty now, having been invited to teach classes in English in exchange for tuition. But she spent her days in a state of misery and gloom—wrestling with her unruly pupils, wandering the Pensionnat grounds in despair—hardly able to concentrate on her studies and future plans. She sorely missed the professor's company and tried hard to understand the change in him. It was only later that she learned that his sudden estrangement was the work of his wife, who had rescheduled his time to keep them apart.

In the summer of 1843, Charlotte Brontë suffered a nervous breakdown. Left alone in the school during the annual five-week-long break, with England far away and the rest of the students and faculty off for vacation or home, Charlotte felt her spirits give way. Feeling more isolated and alone than she had ever felt before, she passed the weeks in a nightmarish daze, roaming the streets of Brussels in anguish and pain.

In December, she left the Pensionnat for good, arriving home so tormented by her love for the professor that she could think of nothing but him. Over the course of the next two years, she wrote him, openly and often, letters that grew increasingly intense as she revealed her true feelings and pleaded for a response. None came.

Those letters, the cries of a passionate and broken heart, so shocked the married man that he cast them away in shreds—shreds that his wife later retrieved and pasted together to read.

In July of 1845, deeply crushed by the professor's

Heger family portrait, 1848

silence, Charlotte was joined in her despair by Branwell, who returned home unexpectedly from Thorp Green. Like Charlotte, he had made the mistake of falling in love with his employer's spouse. But unlike Charlotte, who had recognized the danger and left on her own, Branwell had been dismissed. Anne had preceded Branwell home the month before, too embarrassed by her brother's conduct to stay on with the Robinsons any longer.

The years between 1845 and 1848 saw the rapid decline and slow death of Branwell Brontë. The boy of genius and talent who had shown such promise and cherished such hopes was forever lost to himself and the family who loved him. Pining away for his lost love—mourning anew the deaths of his mother, his two young sisters, his aunt, and his friend—tormented by thoughts of missed chances and shattered dreams—he slowly drugged and drank himself to a certain death, as his father and sisters looked on helplessly.

Only Emily found a way to cope. She would be waiting up for him nights when he stumbled home from the tavern too intoxicated to walk, carrying him in on her back when he could no longer make it on his own. It was a dismal time in the lives of the Brontës, who had known more than their share of suffering, though they tried to struggle on as before. Their one

Branwell's drawing of Thorp Green, where he and Anne taught

hope was the school, "The Misses Brontë's Establishment for Young Ladies," to be set up within the parsonage. Despite Branwell's unsightly state, Charlotte, Emily, and Anne went on with their plans.

With Charlotte in charge, they worked at recruiting students. They sent out fliers, contacted acquaintances and friends, and asked the local townspeople to spread the word. They got no response.

No one came. No one inquired. No one expressed any interest in their school whatsoever. It seemed as if all of their years of preparation and sacrifice had been pointless. But had they?

The flier distributed by the Brontë sisters
for their proposed school

The Misses Bronte's Establishment

FOR

THE BOARD AND EDUCATION

OF A LIMITED NUMBER OF

YOUNG LADIES,

THE PARSONAGE, HAWORTH,

NEAR BRADFORD.

Terms.

	£.	s.	d.
BOARD AND EDUCATION, including Writing, Arithmetic, History, Grammar, Geography, and Needle Work, per Annum, ...	35	0	0
French, .. German, .. Latin .. } .. .. each per Quarter, ...	1	1	0
Music, .. Drawing, .. } .. .. each per Quarter, ...	1	1	0
Use of Piano Forte, per Quarter, ...	0	5	0
Washing, per Quarter, ...	0	15	0

Each Young Lady to be provided with One Pair of Sheets, Pillow Cases, Four Towels, a Dessert and Tea-spoon.

A Quarter's Notice, or a Quarter's Board, is required previous to the Removal of a Pupil.

Having tried and failed to pursue the expected course—with their days of governessing now behind them and their plans for a school by necessity abandoned—the Brontë sisters were finally free to admit the truth.

Teaching was not and never had been their true calling; it was never what they really wanted to do. What they really wanted to do was what they had loved secretly since childhood. Charlotte, Emily, and Anne wanted to write.

chapter seven

Currer, Ellis, and Acton Bell

The year was 1845. Charlotte Brontë, now at home with her sisters for good, unexpectedly chanced upon some poetry of Emily's—strange and wonderful verses that she had not known about before. Confronting Emily with her finding, she soon discovered that Anne, too, had been at work, composing poems of a different and more delicate kind. Putting together the best of their efforts—for Charlotte had also been writing— the three girls published a small collection of verses at their own expense, using money left them by Aunt Branwell. And fearing that the writing of women would not be viewed seriously, they hid their female identities behind pen names. Charlotte Brontë became

Currer Bell, Emily Brontë became Ellis Bell, and Anne Brontë became Acton Bell—pseudonyms that made use of their own initials while remaining deliberately ambiguous as to gender.

But despite their efforts and talent (and two favorable reviews), only two copies sold—a fact that was disappointing but did not deter them from their course. As Charlotte later wrote: "Ill-success failed to crush us; the mere effort to succeed had given a wonderful zest to existence; it must be pursued." With a less-than-satisfying start, the Brontë writing careers had been launched.

They now devoted themselves to novels: Charlotte's *The Professor*, Emily's *Wuthering Heights*, and Anne's *Agnes Grey*—three works that would prove momentous not only in the lives of the Brontë family but also in the history of English literature.

Charlotte's novel, the story of a young Englishwoman in Brussels and her relationship with her teacher, was a fictionalized version of her own experience at the Pensionnat Heger, but with a more satisfying ending. Exercising the novelist's powers to manipulate people and events, she had the hero and heroine of her tale fall in love and marry, and was thus able to achieve in fantasy the happiness that had eluded her in life.

But while the novel is known for its autobiographical content and literary merit, it is even more remarkable for its enlightened views on women. The work was completed in 1846, long before the women's movement had even begun; yet Charlotte's heroine, Frances Henri, is as modern in her thinking as any present-day feminist—determined to pursue her career even after her marriage, questioning the fairness of the superior salaries being offered to men. In Charlotte's time, when a dutiful wife was expected to sacrifice her own interests and goals for the good of her family, and when a woman who worked made less than half as much as her male counterpart, the ideas expressed in this novel were revolutionary.

Anne's work, *Agnes Grey*, was also based on personal experience and, like Charlotte's, also reflected personal views. It is the story of a governess who falls in love and later marries a young curate, and elements of Anne's life are present throughout. Like Anne, Agnes is deeply attached to her family and home but knows that she must leave them to earn her own way. Embarking on a career that requires all her energy and strength, she spends years in service to demanding employers with only her sense of duty and religious beliefs to sustain her.

But unlike Anne, whose love for Willy Weightman remained hidden, Agnes finds fulfillment in marriage. Her story, simply set down and quietly told, is Anne's own, as she might have wished it to be.

Emily's *Wuthering Heights* was very different in content and scope from the works of her sisters. Based on her view of life and the cosmos rather than on her own personal struggles, it tells a tale of eternal love on the moors through the characters of Catherine and Heathcliff, two of the most riveting and powerful in all of literature. Rooted in those early fireside stories of Tabby's and the Gondal writings of childhood, and set completely within her beloved boundaries of home, *Wuthering Heights* is a tale that only Emily could have told—strange, mystical, and as extraordinary and unique as Emily herself.

With the completion of the three novels in July of 1846 came the all-important task of securing a publisher. Charlotte, business-minded and practical, took charge and managed—after twelve months and a series of disheartening rejections—to find acceptance for Emily's and Anne's work, though not for her own. Making one last attempt on her own behalf, she tried the firm of Smith, Elder & Co. in London, and in the summer of 1847 received a response that was both disappointing and hopeful.

Though Smith, Elder had decided against publishing *The Professor*, the firm's reader, William Smith Williams, had been so favorably impressed by Charlotte's talents that he expressed interest in seeing more of her work—specifically a novel in three parts, should she decide to write one. Three-volume works were the favored form of the day. And though Mr. Williams could not have known it when he made such a request, Charlotte already had such a novel under way.

The new work was *Jane Eyre*. It had been started the summer before in the city of Manchester, where Charlotte had taken her father for eye surgery. During the long weeks of his convalescence in the darkened and silent rooms of their lodgings, she had divided her time between attending to his needs and working on her manuscript. By the time the letter from Smith, Elder arrived, Mr. Brontë's eyesight was almost totally restored and Charlotte's novel was just about complete.

She sent it off in August of 1847, and within two months it was not only in print, but was an acclaimed success. Both George Smith, who headed the publishing firm, and Mr. Williams had recognized in an instant its power and worth and had wasted no time in getting it into the public's hands. The story of a governess—poor, plain, but with the integrity and strength of Charlotte Brontë herself—would become the most famous in Victorian England.

Meanwhile, *Wuthering Heights* and *Agnes Grey*, both of which had been accepted long before *Jane Eyre*, had been languishing in the offices of Thomas Newby, their publisher. An unscrupulous man, Thomas Newby had been watching *Jane Eyre*'s success and hatching a plan to cash in on the profits. By suggesting that Currer, Ellis, and Acton Bell were one and the same person and that his firm was holding two more of the author's works, he hoped, when he finally published the novels in December of 1847, to arouse interest and stimulate sales.

But though his deceitful tactics may have been good for business, they caused trouble for Charlotte. George Smith, puzzled by Newby's claims, contacted her for clarification, fearing that she had been dealing with two publishers at once. Too furious at Newby's lie to send Mr. Smith a written response, Charlotte decided that she and her sisters should set off for London at once to show her publisher that there really were three Bells. Unable to convince Emily to go along, she and Anne went alone, arriving at the Smith, Elder offices on July 8, 1848—a momentous day for her and the Smith, Elder staff.

George Smith was thrilled to meet his best-selling author, and relieved to learn that she had not been part of any dishonest plan. And, at Charlotte's request, he

The title pages from the first editions of Charlotte's, Emily's, and Anne's works

graciously agreed to keep the Bells' true identities secret.

Charlotte and Anne spent several pleasant days in London as guests of the Smith family. Though it had been their intention to return to Haworth immediately upon the completion of their business, the kind publisher insisted that they stay on for a while to see the city's sights.

The time passed in a whirl of activities—dinners, parties, visits to museums and galleries, and even an evening at the opera, for which the embarrassed Charlotte and Anne were inappropriately clad, their plain country clothes in marked contrast to the glittering gowns around them. Though Charlotte later complained that the excitement and strain had made her head ache, the attention paid to her and to Anne must have been flattering.

With the publication of *Jane Eyre, Wuthering Heights,* and *Agnes Grey,* the Brontë sisters had more than fulfilled their literary dreams. Not only had they joined the ranks of published authors, but they had also set literary London abuzz with speculation and talk.

Who were these Bells who wrote so brilliantly and remained so obscure?

George Smith knew, as a result of Charlotte and Anne's visit.

And Mary Taylor, now living in New Zealand,

knew, by way of letters from Charlotte.

But no one else, not even Charlotte, Emily, and Anne's closest family members and friends, was at first aware of the truth.

With the same joy in collaboration and secrecy that had characterized their juvenile writing, the three celebrated authors had produced their world-famous works. Gathered round the dining room table each night, with their day's chores complete and the rest of the household in bed and asleep, they had worked on their stories in conspiratorial silence—side by side, deep in thought, occasionally pausing in their writing to read passages to one another aloud. Sharing a common purpose and love—excluding everyone else from their private world—they had slowly rekindled those feelings of closeness they had so cherished in childhood, before outside schooling and work had torn them apart. It was hardly surprising that they should try to keep their activities secret and that they would later attempt to hide their own fame.

Ellen Nussey, however, seems to have discovered the truth on her own. Whether she pieced it together from rumors she heard, or had caught sight of some proof sheets during one of her visits with Charlotte, by the time the public became aware of the identity of the Bells late in 1849, Charlotte's oldest friend already knew. By then, *Jane Eyre* had gone into its third printing, and Charlotte and Anne had each published a second novel—Charlotte's *Shirley*, about an uprising at a Yorkshire cotton mill, and Anne's *The Tenant of Wildfell Hall*, about the evils of drink.

Charlotte did eventually tell her father. One day, about three months after *Jane Eyre* had been published, she approached the man of literature and learning with a copy of her novel and some critical reviews. His eagerly awaited response came later that afternoon at tea.

"Girls," he said, addressing Emily and Anne in Charlotte's presence, "do you know Charlotte has been writing a book, and it is much better than likely?" Imagine his surprise to later learn that they, too, had written for print.

It was only Branwell who never found out. Ravaged by addiction and sadness, Charlotte, Emily, and Anne's beloved brother and childhood collaborator passed from the world without ever knowing of his sisters' fame.

chapter eight

Tragedy Strikes

Branwell Brontë died on September 24, 1848, at the age of thirty-one. He was laid to rest in St. Michael and All Angels Church beside his mother, his sisters, his aunt, and his friend Willy Weightman. Charlotte, sick with grief, spent her brother's funeral day in bed, too ill to attend the services. The day was dark, wet, and thundery—an omen of things to come.

The night after Branwell's burial, Emily fell ill. Drenched during the funeral procession from the parsonage to the church, shivering with cold during the service that followed, she had caught a chill she could not shake. Though she struggled on with her chores in the days and weeks after, refusing to see a doctor or to rest, it was clear from her cough and desperate gasps for air that something was seriously wrong. As the family had helplessly witnessed Branwell's slow death from despair, they now watched in horror as tuberculosis destroyed Emily.

Like the cholera that had taken Willy Weightman's life, tuberculosis was an ever-present danger. Mr. Brontë, a crusader for better sanitation in the town, had long advocated a change in its water and sewage system. Because Haworth had no indoor plumbing and no organized means for the disposal of waste, its main street was often overflowing with debris.

Even worse, the Brontës' own water supply came from a well located in the parsonage graveyard, where the bacteria from decaying bodies could easily seep through. It is not surprising that they were often ill with fevers and colds and that years of unhealthy living conditions would tragically take their toll.

But it was also clear from Emily's refusal to rest or seek help that something more than a physical ailment was at work. Emily wanted to die. Unable to cope with her sadness, she saw death as a way to escape from her grief. Not even Charlotte and Anne, who knew her best, understood what was wrong.

Desperate to cheer her—frantic to rekindle those fading sparks of life—Charlotte scoured the moors on the cold winter morning of Emily's demise, searching for one last sprig of autumn heather. Finding one, she placed it tenderly on Emily's pillow, then watched in sadness as her sister gazed with unseeing eyes on the flower she had loved.

Emily Brontë died on December 19, 1848, at the age of thirty. Her old friend Tabby, now nearing ninety and lame, was among her mourners. Her faithful dog Keeper, who crouched quietly in the family pew for the entire length of the service, howled pitifully at her bedroom door for days after.

Almost immediately after Emily's death, Anne became ill, suffering from the same alarming symptoms that had signaled trouble for Emily. Charlotte and her father were beside themselves with worry. Still reeling from their double loss, they now had to face the possibility that Anne, too, would die. Their one consolation was Anne's willingness to seek help. Unlike Emily, who had rejected their pleas for medical care, Anne obediently submitted to the instructions of her doctor. Bravely and uncomplainingly, she put herself through the unpleasant treatments of the time, including medicines that were so nauseating they made it impossible for her to eat. But nothing worked.

Believing that a change of atmosphere might help, Charlotte and Ellen arranged to take Anne to

Emily's watercolor of her dog Keeper

Scarborough, a village on the northeastern coast of England, for a spell of sea air. It was there on a sofa overlooking the bay that she died on May 28, 1849. She was twenty-nine.

Sparing Mr. Brontë the pain of yet another funeral

and burial, the two friends laid Anne to rest in the Scarborough churchyard. Though Ellen wanted to accompany Charlotte home afterward, Charlotte insisted on returning to Haworth alone, hardly braced for the overwhelming silence that greeted her. Two days later, she wrote Ellen:

> I got home a little before eight o'clock. All was clean and bright waiting for me—Papa and the servants were well—and all received me with an affection which should have consoled. . . .

> I left Papa soon and went into the dining-room—I shut the door—I tried to be glad that I was come home . . . but this time joy was not to be the sensation. I felt that the house was all silent—the rooms were all empty—I remembered where the three were laid—in what narrow dark dwellings—never were they to reappear on earth. . . .

> . . . The great trial is when evening closes and night approaches—At that hour we used to assemble in the dining-room—we used to talk—Now I sit by myself—necessarily I am silent—

Anne Brontë's grave in Scarborough

I cannot help thinking of their last days—
remembering their sufferings and what they
said and did, and how they looked in mortal
affliction—perhaps all this will be less poi-
gnant in time.

But it never was.

chapter nine

The Famous Author

The year before Emily's death, Charlotte had started work on her third novel, *Shirley*. Unable to write during those terrible months of her sister's decline, she had put the manuscript aside, too heartsick to go on. The intense involvement with words that had seen her through so many difficult times in the past was of little comfort to her then; part of her creative energy and spirit was dying with her sister.

Finding little joy in the occupation that had once given her such pleasure, yet determined not to give in to her despair, Charlotte forced herself to resume work the month after Emily's death. Much of the task was painful, for in many ways the title character of Shirley was a literary portrait of Emily.

The novel, completed in August of 1849, was, like *Jane Eyre* before it, an instant and resounding success. Once again Charlotte found herself showered with praise. Mail poured into the quiet parsonage: admiring letters from readers, glowing reviews forwarded by her publisher, appreciative notes from the famous authors and critics of the day. Literary London was beckoning, and Charlotte, grief-stricken and lonely, responded. Where she had once recoiled in terror from outside contact, she now welcomed the chance to escape the gloom of the parsonage and join the lively London scene.

In late November of 1849, she set off for England's capital. Though she was now familiar with the city and the kindness of her publisher-host, she was still painfully shy and miserably ill at ease. Doing his best to make her feel welcome, George Smith arranged to accompany her on another round of visits to museums, galleries, theaters, and famous sights. He also introduced her to her literary idols, the novelist William Makepeace Thackeray and the social reformer and writer Harriet Martineau. There was nothing she might wish for that he wouldn't willingly provide. Although he was kind, he was also aware that much of his own success depended on Charlotte.

Tall, handsome and, at twenty-five, eight years

Charlotte's junior, George Smith had inherited the Smith, Elder firm in 1846. Determined to raise the company to a place of prominence, he had been searching for a promising new writer and an exciting new work. In Currer Bell he had found his author, and in *Jane Eyre* and *Shirley* he had not one but two best-selling books. It is not surprising that he treated Charlotte like the celebrity she had become.

After an exhilarating and exhausting two-week-long stay, Charlotte returned home to a parsonage that seemed more desolate than ever. Never had the hall clock ticked so loudly. Never had her father appeared more withdrawn.

Old now and often ill, Mr. Brontë was spending virtually all of his time alone, leaving Charlotte to pass her days in solitary silence. When he did join her for the occasional tea, he fussed so over her health that their time together was far from pleasant. And it was only natural that he should worry, when his only surviving child seemed so increasingly prone to severe fevers and colds.

But what Charlotte lacked in companionship and health, she more than made up for in correspondence. Mail was still her great joy, a happy reminder of her many old and new friends.

Mary Taylor wrote from New Zealand with news

George Smith, around the time that Charlotte Brontë knew him

of life in that rough and distant land.

William Smith Williams sent packages of the latest books.

And Ellen, faithful as ever, kept in close and constant touch.

But through all of those tragic and triumphant years between 1845 and 1849, there was one loyal and silent friend of whom Charlotte was scarcely aware. Arthur Bell Nicholls, the curate who had come to assist Mr. Brontë in Willy Weightman's place and who had secretly applauded her achievements and quietly suffered her pain, was waiting anxiously for the day when he could finally reveal his love.

The Reverend Arthur Bell Nicholls—born, raised, and educated in Ireland—had accepted the Haworth position in 1845. Serious and principled, he had performed his clerical duties with devotion and skill. Even more to his credit, he had stood by the Brontë family through their many times of trouble.

But despite his kindness and strength, Charlotte found him narrow-minded and dull—hardly the kind of man she could care for or love. He had none of Willy Weightman's charm. He possessed none of Monsieur Heger's fiery spirit. And he was nothing at all like George Smith. With her romantic sights now set on London, Charlotte barely gave him a thought.

In May of 1850, she made her third trip to the city, once again as George's guest. Eager to please him, she agreed to sit for a crayon portrait by George Richmond, a famous artist of the time. She would have done anything to win the affection of her publisher, to whom she felt increasingly drawn. What she couldn't do was be beautiful. Nonetheless, she would try.

The following year, in preparation for her fourth London visit, she spent a day in nearby Leeds shopping for dress material and a hat. She gazed longingly at the pretty pastels, fingered the fancy bonnets adorned with flowers and lace, and tried to break free from her conservative ties. But after long deliberation, she finally settled on plain black silk for the dress and a simple black bonnet. She did, however, allow herself the indulgence of pink lining for the hat, a daring and touchingly feminine choice for the practical Charlotte.

In between the two London visits, she spent three days in Scotland as a guest of George Smith and his sister. In a letter afterward, she told Ellen that it was the happiest she had been in some time.

But it was becoming painfully clear, as the hours she and George spent together increased, that his interest in her was far from romantic. She realized that in spite of their mutual regard, they could never be more than colleagues and friends. In one heart-wrenching

The Reverend Arthur Bell Nicholls

George Richmond's crayon portrait of Charlotte

blow, Charlotte put an end to their personal association. To George's suggestion of a fifth London visit, at the end of the year, Charlotte said no.

In November of 1851, she began work on her fourth novel, *Villette*. Into her most autobiographical tale, she poured all of her disappointments and hopes. Through her heroine, Lucy Snowe, she told her own story of love and loss, transforming her publisher into the young and handsome Dr. John and her former professor into Monsieur Paul Emanuel, Lucy's teacher. The novel was well received. Her place in the literary establishment was secure.

Among the many friends Charlotte made during this period of her greatest fame, perhaps none was more important than Elizabeth Gaskell. Charlotte had met the short-story writer and novelist through one of her devoted fans. Intelligent, warmhearted, and kind, Mrs. Gaskell was the perfect confidant for the brilliant and lonely author. She shared Charlotte's passion for literature and writing and was equally committed to the female cause. She was also a sympathetic listener. Charlotte could talk to her about her life, her work, and the tragedies she had endured. Charlotte visited with her often, both at Mrs. Gaskell's Manchester home and at the home of a mutual friend. She also invited her to Haworth. When Mrs. Gaskell finally came, in

September of 1853, the mood at the parsonage became a good bit less bleak.

The months prior to Mrs. Gaskell's visit had been especially trying.

In December of 1852, Arthur Bell Nicholls had finally proposed, an act of courage and love that had surprised and touched Charlotte but had horrified her father. Terrified of losing her, Mr. Brontë had railed against his loyal curate, said he was unworthy of his daughter's hand, and accused him of pursuing Charlotte for her literary income and fame.

Although Charlotte had no intention of marrying Reverend Nicholls, she was grieved by her father's harshness. She knew, only too well, how it felt to love without hope. Over the course of the next sixteen months, as she saw the depth of the curate's affection and despair, she found herself growing sympathetic to his plight.

Did she come to love the man she had at first intended to reject? Did she realize that at thirty-seven her prospects for marriage to anyone else were dim? Or had news of George Smith's own marriage convinced her? No one really knows. But in April of 1854, Charlotte Brontë agreed to become Arthur's wife.

Charlotte and Arthur were married on June 29, 1854, in a quiet ceremony in the Haworth church.

Wearing a simple white dress and bonnet, Charlotte was joined by Miss Wooler and Ellen—her only guests. Mr. Brontë did not attend. To commemorate the day, she planted two small fir trees in front of her home.

The couple honeymooned in Ireland, where Charlotte met her husband's family and explored her ancestral homeland. She was favorably impressed by both. Only a stubborn cough and cold spoiled her pleasure.

In August, the newlyweds returned to the parsonage, where in consideration of Mr. Brontë they had decided to live.

Now a busy wife as well as a caring daughter, Charlotte found herself in constant demand. What precious moments she had, she put into the start of a new novel, called *Emma*.

If she sometimes resented the incessant pull on her time—if she sometimes wished for a husband who was more literary and poetic—she at least had the satisfaction of knowing she was loved.

One day in November of 1854 as she was writing to Ellen, Arthur asked her to join him for a walk. Eager to please him, she put down her pen, and they set off together for a distant waterfall. During their return, they were caught in a sudden downpour, which soaked them to the skin. Within hours, Charlotte was ill, and four months later she was dead.

chapter ten

A Family Called Brontë

Despite her fame, Charlotte Brontë had lived her final years in relative obscurity, far removed from the literary and social scene. Though her books had continued to be great favorites, her readers and fans had known little about her. With her death came a renewed interest in the details of her life and a new round of speculation and talk. So much of what was written and said was false that Ellen, grieved and angered by the untruths, searched for a way to set them right.

In June of 1855, she approached Mr. Brontë about a biography of Charlotte. He was, at first, reluctant to expose his daughter's life to public view, but the continuing inaccuracies began to trouble him, too. In

July he engaged Elizabeth Gaskell to write the story of Charlotte's life. He couldn't have made a better choice.

Sensitive, thoughtful, written with love and great skill, Mrs. Gaskell's work is a tribute to Charlotte's spirit and genius. It is also the only biography of this extraordinary woman to be written by someone who knew her. Published in March of 1857 by Charlotte's own Smith, Elder and Co., *The Life of Charlotte Brontë* was an instant success. It remains to this day an important source of information on the famous writer and her family.

With interest in Charlotte running high, 1857 also saw the publication of *The Professor*, Charlotte's novel from ten years back that had never made it to print. Understanding the importance of the work to Brontë scholars and fans, Arthur Nicholls composed a short foreword to the book, which Smith, Elder was pleased to include.

The unfinished *Emma*—fifty pages in length at Charlotte's death—was published as a fragment in George Smith's *Cornhill Magazine* in the spring of 1860. Although it was similar to *Jane Eyre* in approach and mood, we can only guess at where Charlotte's pen, had it continued to flow, would have taken it. Its author would no doubt have been pleased to know that William Makepeace Thackeray, her London friend and literary idol, had written the introduction.

Ellen Nussey, loyal to the end, devoted the rest of her life to Charlotte's memory, sharing letters and reminiscences with all who were interested. Outliving Charlotte by forty-two years, she died in 1897 at the age of eighty.

Mr. Brontë spent his final years in the care of Arthur Bell Nicholls, who, true to a promise he had made Charlotte, stayed on at the parsonage until his father-in-law's death in 1861 at the age of eighty-four. With the last member of the famous family gone, the parsonage graveyard and crypt, the source of so much of their sickness and grief, were sealed up forever.

Arthur Nicholls gathered together the remaining mementos of the family's life, including Charlotte's portrait, her letters, two diary notes of Emily's and Anne's, and the tiny childhood books, and returned to his native Ireland. He worked as a farmer until his death in 1906.

A new century had dawned. And an era in the history of the Brontë family had both ended and begun.

In the decades since, the Brontë story has become legendary, and the Brontë works are now ranked among the world's classics. Published in numerous English-language and foreign editions, the novels have

Patrick Brontë in old age

also been adapted for production on television, radio, film, and stage.

The parsonage, virtually uninhabited since Mr. Brontë's demise, was opened to the public in 1928. Now a museum that attracts thousands of visitors each year, it is under the loving care and watchful eye of the Brontë Society—an organization dedicated to the perpetuation of the Brontë name—and remains very much the home the family knew.

In addition to many of the original furnishings and artifacts, it houses the Bonnell Collection, an assemblage of Brontë manuscripts and drawings that had been sold and scattered throughout the world in the years before Arthur Nicholls's death. Gathered together by Henry Houston Bonnell, an American collector and Brontë enthusiast, the treasures were donated to the museum in 1929 and form the heart of its holdings. The museum also displays articles of clothing, jewelry, writing materials, and books once belonging to the family.

So real are the parsonage surroundings, so little touched by the passage of time, that a trip to the site is an eerie walk back in history, a rendezvous with the strange and distant Brontë past. Visitors say that if you close your eyes and listen hard, you can almost hear the rustle of Aunt Branwell's skirts on the stairs and the

The Brontë Parsonage Museum today

voices of Charlotte, Branwell, Emily, and Anne calling to one another across the moors.

Universal despite their Yorkshire ties—immortal despite their corporeal passing—the Brontë family has left a legacy of achievement and courage that defies the boundaries of space and time. In their Haworth home, in their story of tragedy and fame, and in the stunning works that remain behind, the Brontë name thunders on.

Charlotte, Emily, and Anne

Selected Poems

Notes for "Parting"
by
Charlotte Brontë

Charlotte wrote this poem in January of 1838 as she was preparing to return to Miss Wooler's after the Christmas holidays. Sad to be leaving home, she tries to comfort herself and her family through the power of thought and the hope of happier times to come.

Parting

There's no use in weeping,
    Though we are condemned to part;
There's such a thing as keeping
    A remembrance in one's heart:

There's such a thing as dwelling
    On the thought ourselves have nursed,
And with scorn and courage telling
    The world to do its worst.

We'll not let its follies grieve us,
    We'll just take them as they come;
And then every day will leave us
    A merry laugh for home.

When we've left each friend and brother,
    When we're parted, wide and far,
We will think of one another,
    As even better than we are.

Every glorious sight above us,.
    Every pleasant sight beneath,
We'll connect with those that love us,
    Whom we truly love till death!

In the evening, when we're sitting
    By the fire, perchance alone,
Then shall heart with warm heart meeting,
    Give responsive tone for tone.

We can burst the bonds which chain us,
    Which cold human hands have wrought,
And where none shall dare restrain us
    We can meet again, in thought.

So there's no use in weeping,
    Bear a cheerful spirit still:
Never doubt that Fate is keeping
    Future good for present ill!

Notes for "A Valentine"
by
Charlotte Brontë

This lighthearted verse was written in February of 1840 in response to Willy Weightman's valentines. Though the poem is credited to Charlotte, it was really a joint effort by Charlotte, Emily, Anne, and Ellen Nussey, who was visiting at the time and had also received a token of Willy's love. Besides offering thanks, it lets Willy know that his young admirers believe him destined for greatness. His "doom," or fate, will be a glorious one beyond the lonely Yorkshire moors.

The expression "A Roland for your Oliver" in the opening line means an equal exchange: in this case, a poem for the four valentines. The expression comes from the story of Roland and Oliver, two 8th-century knights who were equals in combat and who later became friends.

A Valentine

A Roland for your Oliver
    We think you've justly earned;
You sent us such a valentine,
    Your gift is now returned.

We cannot write or talk like you;
    We're plain folks every one;
You've played a clever jest on us,
    We thank you for the fun.

Believe us when we frankly say
    (Our words, though blunt, are true),
At home, abroad, by night or day,
    We all wish well to you.

And never may a cloud come o'er
    The sunshine of your mind;
Kind friends, warm hearts, and happy hours
    Through life, we trust, you'll find.

Where'er you go, however far
    In future years you stray,
There shall not want our earnest prayer
    To speed you on your way.

A stranger and a pilgrim here
    We know you sojourn now;
But brighter hopes, with brighter wreaths,
    Are doomed to bind your brow.

Not always in these lonely hills
    Your humble lot shall lie;
The oracle of fate foretells
    A worthier destiny.

And though her words are veiled in gloom,
    Though clouded her decree,
Yet doubt not that a juster doom
    She keeps in store for thee.

Then cast hope's anchor near the shore,
    'Twill hold your vessel fast,
And fear not for the tide's deep roar,
    And dread not for the blast.

For though this station now seems near,
    'Mid land-locked creeks to be,
The helmsman soon his ship will steer
    Out to the wide blue sea.

Well officered and staunchly manned,
    Well built to meet the blast;
With favouring winds the bark must land
    On glorious shores at last.

Notes for "I'm Happiest When Most Away"
by
Emily Brontë

Though this is thought to be a fragment rather than a
finished poem, it captures in its eight beautifully crafted
lines the very essence of a mystical experience.

I'm Happiest When Most Away

I'm happiest when most away
I can bear my soul from its home of clay
On a windy night when the moon is bright
And the eye can wander through worlds of light—

When I am not and none beside—
Nor earth nor sea nor cloudless sky—
But only spirit wandering wide
Through infinite immensity.

Notes for "The Old Stoic"
by
Emily Brontë

In this poem, which may have been Gondal in origin, Emily expresses her strong feelings about freedom and courage. Her most famous verse, its last four words are inscribed on the Brontë memorial in London's Westminster Abbey.

The Old Stoic

Riches I hold in light esteem
And Love I laugh to scorn
And lust of Fame was but a dream
That vanished with the morn—

And if I pray, the only prayer
That moves my lips for me
Is—'Leave the heart that now I bear
And give me liberty.'

Yes, as my swift days near their goal
'Tis all that I implore—
Through life and death a chainless soul
With courage to endure!

Notes for "Night"
by
Anne Brontë

Like Emily's "The Old Stoic," this poem of Anne's may also have been Gondal in origin. Written in March of 1845, it seems to express her continuing grief over the death of Willy Weightman.

Night

I love the silent hour of night,
For blissful dreams may then arise,
Revealing to my charméd sight
What may not bless my waking eyes!

And then a voice may meet my ear
That death has silenced long ago;
And hope and rapture may appear
Instead of solitude and woe.

Cold in the grave for years has lain
The form it was my bliss to see,
And only dreams can bring again
The darling of my heart to me.

Notes for "Home"
by
Anne Brontë

In these lines, probably written during her employment at Thorp Green, Anne contrasts the beauty of the Thorp Green setting to the barrenness of Haworth. Though she admits that Haworth is colder, grayer, and far less appealing to the eye, she prefers it and longs to return home.

Home

How brightly glistening in the sun
    The woodland ivy plays!
While yonder beeches from their barks
    Reflect his silver rays.

That sun surveys a lovely scene
    From softly smiling skies;
And wildly through unnumbered trees
    The wind of winter sighs:

Now loud, it thunders o'er my head,
    And now in distance dies.
But give me back my barren hills
    Where colder breezes rise;

Where scarce the scattered, stunted trees
  Can yield an answering swell,
But where a wilderness of heath
  Returns the sound as well.

For yonder garden, fair and wide,
  With groves of evergreen,
Long winding walks, and borders trim,
  And velvet lawns between;

Restore to me that little spot,
  With gray walls compassed round,
Where knotted grass neglected lies,
  And weeds usurp the ground.

Though all around this mansion high
  Invites the foot to roam,
And though its halls are fair within—
  Oh, give me back my home!

Chronology

1777   Patrick (Brunty) Brontë is born in Ireland.

1783   Maria Branwell (the future Mrs. Brontë) is born in Penzance, England.

1802   Patrick leaves Ireland for England.

1802-
1806   Patrick studies theology at Cambridge University. He changes the family name.

1806   Patrick is ordained a minister in the Church of England.

1812   Patrick and Maria meet and marry.

1813   Maria Brontë is born in Hartshead.

1815   Elizabeth Brontë is born in Hartshead.

1816   Charlotte Brontë is born in Thornton on April 21.

1817   Branwell Brontë is born in Thornton on June 26.

1818   Emily Brontë is born in Thornton on July 30.

1820   Anne Brontë is born in Thornton on January 17. The Brontë family moves to Haworth in April.

1821   Mrs. Brontë falls ill. Elizabeth ("Aunt") Branwell arrives from Penzance. Mrs. Brontë dies.

1824-
1825 Maria, Elizabeth, Charlotte, and Emily attend the Clergy Daughters' School at Cowan Bridge.

1825 Maria and Elizabeth die. Charlotte and Emily leave Cowan Bridge. Tabitha ("Tabby") Aykroyd arrives at the parsonage.

1826 Branwell receives a gift of toy soldiers. The Brontë children begin their Glasstown saga.

1831-
1832 Charlotte attends Miss Wooler's school at Roe Head.

1835-
1838 Charlotte teaches at Roe Head; first Emily and then Anne attend as students. Branwell travels to London to study at the Royal Academy, but fails to enroll. Emily teaches at Law Hill. Branwell settles in Bradford as a portrait painter.

1839 Branwell returns from Bradford. Charlotte and Anne become governesses for the Sidgwicks and Inghams, respectively. William Weightman arrives in Haworth.

1840 Branwell works as a tutor, then a railway clerk. Anne becomes governess for the Robinson family at Thorp Green.

1841 Charlotte works as a governess for the Whites. She informs her family of her plans to establish a school.

1842   Charlotte and Emily enroll at the Pensionnat Heger in Brussels. Branwell is dismissed by the railway company. William Weightman and Aunt Branwell die. Charlotte and Emily return from Brussels in November.

1843   Charlotte goes back to Brussels alone, but leaves in December. Branwell joins Anne at Thorp Green.

1845   Arthur Bell Nicholls arrives in Haworth. Anne and Branwell return from Thorp Green. Charlotte, Emily, and Anne are unsuccessful in their attempts to establish a school; each begins a novel. Charlotte discovers Emily's poems and suggests joint publication.

1846   *Poems* by Currer, Ellis, and Acton Bell is published. *The Professor, Wuthering Heights,* and *Agnes Grey* are completed. Charlotte begins *Jane Eyre.*

1847   *Wuthering Heights* and *Agnes Grey* are accepted for publication; *The Professor* is rejected. *Jane Eyre* is accepted by Smith, Elder and published in October. *Wuthering Heights* and *Agnes Grey* are published by Newby in December. Anne begins *The Tenant of Wildfell Hall,* and Charlotte begins *Shirley.*

1848   Charlotte and Anne travel to London. *The Tenant of Wildfell Hall* is published. Branwell dies on September 24. Emily dies on December 19.

1849   Anne dies on May 28. *Shirley* is published in October. Charlotte goes to London for the second time.

1850-   Charlotte makes two more trips to London. She
1851   meets Elizabeth Gaskell and begins *Villette*.

1852   Arthur Bell Nicholls proposes.

1853   *Villette* is published.

1854   Charlotte accepts Arthur's proposal in April and marries him in June. She begins *Emma*.

1855   Charlotte dies on March 31. Elizabeth Gaskell begins *The Life of Charlotte Brontë*.

1857   *The Life of Charlotte Brontë* and *The Professor* are published.

1861   Patrick Brontë dies. Arthur Bell Nicholls returns to Ireland.

1906   Arthur Bell Nicholls dies.

1928   The Brontë parsonage becomes the Brontë Parsonage Museum.

Selected Bibliography

Alexander, Christine. *The Early Writings of Charlotte Brontë*. Buffalo, New York: Prometheus Books, 1983.

Barker, Juliet R. V., ed. *The Brontës: Selected Poems*. London: J. M. Dent, 1985.

Bentley, Phyllis. *The Brontës*. New York: Thames and Hudson, 1986.

Brontë, Anne. *Agnes Grey*. London: J. M. Dent, 1982.

_____.*The Tenant of Wildfell Hall*. Oxford: Shakespeare Head Press, 1931.

Brontë, Charlotte. *Jane Eyre*. New York: Random House, 1950.

_____.*The Professor*. London: J. M. Dent, 1965.

_____.*The Secret & Lily Hart*. Columbia: University of Missouri Press, 1979.

_____.*Shirley*. London: J. M. Dent, 1965.

_____.*Villette*. London: J. M. Dent, 1974.

Brontë, Emily. *Wuthering Heights*. New York: Random House, 1950.

Brontë Newsletter. Oradell, New Jersey. Numerous articles from 1982 to 1987.

Brontë Society Transactions. Keighley, England. Numerous articles from 1981 to 1987.

Chitham, Edward, and Tom Winnifrith. *Selected Brontë Poems*. Oxford: Basil Blackwell, 1985.

Craik, W. A. *The Brontë Novels*. London: Methuen, 1968.

Crandall, Norma Rand. *Emily Brontë: A Psychological Portrait*. Rindge, New Hampshire: R. R. Smith, 1957.

Davies, Stevie. *The Brontë Sisters: Selected Poems of Charlotte, Emily and Anne Brontë*. Cheshire, England: Carcanet Press, 1976.

Fraser, Rebecca. *The Brontës: Charlotte Brontë and Her Family*. New York: Crown Publishers, 1988.

Gaskell, Elizabeth. *The Life of Charlotte Brontë*. Middlesex, England: Penguin Books, 1983.

Gerin, Winifred. *Anne Brontë*. London: Thomas Nelson and Sons, 1959.

_____. *Branwell Brontë*. London: Thomas Nelson and Sons, 1961.

_____. *Charlotte Brontë: The Evolution of Genius*. London: Oxford University Press, 1967.

_____. *Emily Brontë*. London: Oxford University Press, 1978.

Gregor, Ian, ed. *The Brontës: A Collection of Critical Essays*. Englewood Cliffs, New Jersey: Prentice-Hall, 1970.

Hatfield, C. W., ed. *The Complete Poems of Emily Jane Brontë*. New York: Columbia University Press, 1941.

Hopkins, Annette B. *The Father of the Brontës*. Baltimore: The Johns Hopkins Press, 1958.

Lane, Margaret. *The Brontë Story: A Reconsideration of Mrs. Gaskell's "Life of Charlotte Brontë."* Westport, Connecticut: Greenwood Press, 1971.

Lewis, Naomi, ed. *Emily Brontë: A Peculiar Music*. New York: Macmillan, 1971.

Maurat, Charlotte. *The Brontës' Secret*. London: Constable, 1969.

O'Neill, Judith, ed. *Critics on Charlotte and Emily Brontë*. Coral Gables, Florida: University of Miami Press, 1968.

Peters, Margot. *Charlotte Brontë: Style in the Novel*. Madison: University of Wisconsin Press, 1973.

_____.*Unquiet Soul: A Biography of Charlotte Brontë*. New York: Atheneum, 1986.

Peters, Maureen. *An Enigma of Brontës*. New York: St. Martin's Press, 1974.

Pollard, Arthur. *The Landscape of the Brontës*. New York: E. P. Dutton, 1988.

Ratchford, Fannie. *The Brontës' Web of Childhood*. New York: Russell and Russell, 1964.

_____.*Gondal's Queen*. Austin: University of Texas Press, 1955.

Shorter, Clement. *The Brontës and Their Circle*. New York: E. P. Dutton, 1970.

Spark, Muriel. *The Brontë Letters*. London: Macmillan, 1966.

Wilks, Brian. *The Brontës*. London: Hamlyn, 1975.

Willy, Margaret. *A Critical Commentary on Wuthering Heights*. New York: Macmillan, 1966.

Winnifrith, Tom. *The Brontës*. New York: Macmillan, 1977.

Woolf, Virginia. "Jane Eyre and *Wuthering Heights*." In *The Common Reader*, First Series. London: Hogarth Press, 1933.

Index

Sources of Illustrations

On the cover: portrait of Charlotte Brontë, by J. H. Thompson, photographed by Simon Warner, © the Brontë Society; portrait of Anne Brontë, by Charlotte Brontë, photographed by Simon Warner, © the Brontë Society; portrait of Emily Brontë, by Branwell Brontë, © National Portrait Gallery, London.
Back cover image courtesy of Simon Warner

Haworth parsonage and church, by Elizabeth Gaskell, for her *Life of Charlotte Brontë*, photographed by N. K. Howarth, © the Brontë Society—pages 10-11

Patrick Brontë as a young man, artist unknown, photographed by Simon Warner, © the Brontë Society—page 13

Patrick Brontë's birthplace, artist unknown, photographed by N. K. Howarth, © the Brontë Society—page 14

Maria Branwell, by J. Tonkins, photographed by N. K. Howarth, © the Brontë Society—page 16

The Brontë home in Thornton, photographed by N. K. Howarth, © the Brontë Society—page 18

The parsonage at Haworth, photographed by N. K. Howarth, © the Brontë Society—page 20

The Haworth moors, photographed by Simon Warner—pages 22-23

The parsonage dining room, photographed by Simon Warner, © the Brontë Society—page 25

Silhouette of Aunt Branwell, artist unknown, photographed by Simon Warner, © the Brontë Society—page 27

The Clergy Daughters' School, by O. Jewitt, photographed by N. K. Howarth, © the Brontë Society—page 29

The juvenile books, photographed by Simon Warner, © the Brontë Society—page 33

"English Lady," by Charlotte Brontë, photographed by N. K. Howarth, © the Brontë Society—page 36

The Duke of Zamorna, by Branwell Brontë, photographed by N. K. Howarth, © the Brontë Society—page 38